Making a Difference

REUSING
Things

Sue Barraclough

SEA-TO-SEA
Mankato Collingwood London

This edition first published in 2008 by
Sea-to-Sea Publications
1980 Lookout Drive
North Mankato
Minnesota 56003

Library of Congress
Cataloging in Publication Data

Barraclough, Sue.
   Reusing things / by Sue Barraclough
      p.cm. -- (Making a difference)
   ISBN 978-1-59771-109-8
   1. Environmental protection--Citizen participation--Juvenile literature. 2.
Recycling (Waste, etc.)--Juvenile literature. I. Title

TD171.7.B37 2007
363.72'82--dc22

                                              2006051277

9 8 7 6 5 4 3

Published by arrangement with the Watts Publishing Group Ltd, London.

Original concept devised by
Sue Barraclough and Jemima Lumley.

Editor: Adrian Cole
Designer: Jemima Lumley
Art director: Jonathan Hair
Special photography: Mark Simmons (except where listed below)
Consultant: Helen Peake, Education Officer at
   The Recycling Consortium, Bristol

Acknowledgments:
The author and publisher wish to thank Helen Peake and the staff at
The Recycling Consortium. Green Glass (www.greenglass.co.uk); page 27.
The Recycling Consortium; page 25tr. Images on pages 8, 9, 18b, 19br, 20,
23t, 26l supplied by the national Recycle Now campaign (for more
information on recycling visit www.recyclenow.com). Topfoto Syracuse
Newspapers/Image Works/Topfoto; page 21b.

Special thanks to Connie, James, Romi, Ruby, and Tom for taking part.

Contents

Is it really garbage?

Some garbage can be reused.
We can use, repair, or make
it into something else.

An old chair (see page 15)

A pile of junk (see page 12)

Used paper (see page 10)

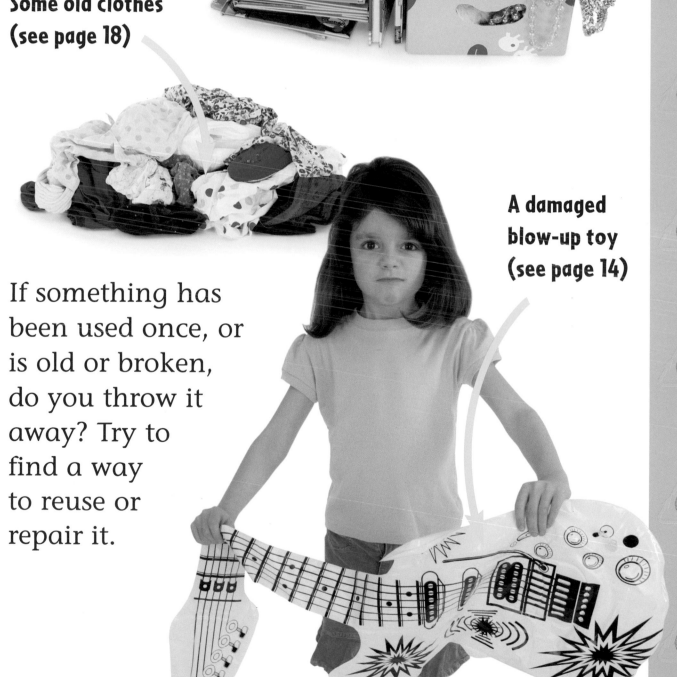

**Some old
books and toys
(see page 16)**

**Some old clothes
(see page 18)**

**A damaged
blow-up toy
(see page 14)**

If something has
been used once, or
is old or broken,
do you throw it
away? Try to
find a way
to reuse or
repair it.

Why reuse?

Most of the garbage we throw away
is collected and buried
in big holes called landfill sites.
One day there will not be any more
space to bury our garbage.

When we reuse things, less
garbage is buried in landfill sites.

Reusing something makes
the most of the time, money,
materials, and energy used
to make it.

Reusing paper

There are lots of ways to reuse paper. One of the easiest ways to make the best use of paper is to use both sides. Use scrap paper for lists, doodles, and to make other things.

Used paper

Make a paper plane

**Make a notepad
or book**

**Print your own
wrapping paper**

**Create a
paper collage**

**What
you can do**

Make gift tags
from old birthday
or Christmas cards.

11

Reusing junk

Reuse packaging and junk to make things. Use all the different materials, shapes, and patterns to make a monster model!

Look at all these ways of using something again.

Jamjar pencil pot

Plastic bottle funnel

Can you think of more ways to reuse a piece of junk?

Egg carton organizer

Repair and repaint

Sometimes toys, like this blow-up guitar, are easy to repair. Ask an adult to help you glue, sew, or patch it.

Repair

Other things, like this chair, can be repaired and repainted. Ask an adult to help you.

An old chair

This chair was painted and decorated to make it look better.

Borrow and give away

Another way to reuse is to borrow books and toys from a library. Then you can take them back and get some different ones.

If you are bored with your toys or books, do not put them in the garbage.

Pack them up and give them away to someone else, or take them to a goodwill store.

What you can do

Give away books that you are too old for, or that you no longer read.

Old clothes?

Do not throw old clothes into the garbage. There are lots of ways you can reuse them.

Put them into a clothes bank or take them to a goodwill store

Renew clothes by adding patches and other decorations

Wear an old shirt as an overall for messy jobs

Did you know?

Millions of people around the world are too poor to buy the clothes and shoes they need.

Buy second-hand

Another way to reuse things is to buy second-hand clothes and toys. You can give the goodwill store something you are bored with, and buy something that is new to you.

You can help sort out your family's old clothes to take to a yard sale.

What you can do

Look for garage or yard sales in your neighborhood. They are a great place to find new toys.

Reusing bags

Plastic bags are lightweight and strong. They are good for carrying shopping, but bad for our world. Plastic bags can easily blow away and pollute our countryside.

When you help unpack the groceries, do not throw the bags away. Reuse them next time. Try using strong plastic bags that are made to be reused.

Cloth bags, cardboard boxes, or a basket can also be reused to carry groceries.

What you can do

Make tiny bag bundles to put in your pocket. Then you will have a bag when you need one.

Choose to reuse

Many things are made to be thrown away once you have used them. Think of disposable diapers, plastic cups, bottles, and throw-away cameras.

We should choose things
that are made to last
and can be reused.

Some diapers
can be reused

A plastic lunchbox
can be reused

Dangerous waste
Choose batteries
that can be
reused and help reduce
the dangerous waste sent
to landfill sites.
Only special
batteries
can be
recharged.

25

What's been reused?

Can you tell what has
been reused to make
each object?

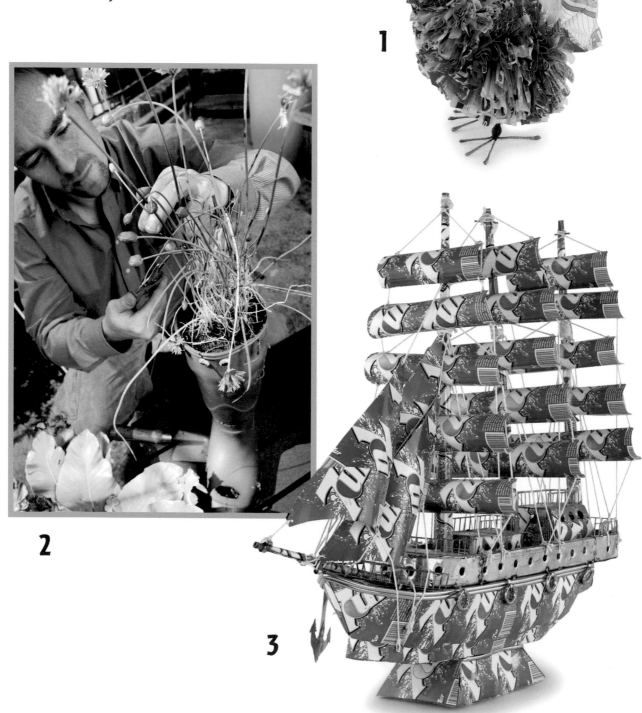

1

2

3

4

5

6

Answers on
page 29.

Find out more

Reusing things means you will send less garbage to landfill sites. Before you throw something into a trash can, think of a way you can reuse it, or store it somewhere for when you need it. This way you will make the best use of the time, money, energy, and materials used to make it.

www.make-stuff.com
A good website for ideas on reusing household items to make things.

www.childrensscrapstore. co.uk
Find out where you can find reusable art and craft resources in your area.

www.planetark.com/ campaignspage.cfm
Click on "plastic bags— just say no" to find out more about this campaign in Australia.

http://scrap-sf.org/ links.htm
Some great links from the Scroungers' Center for Reusable Art Parts!

www.recyclenow.com
Type "reusing" in the search box to discover lots of ideas on reusing and recycling.

www.reusablebags.com
All about reusable bags and other reusable items.

www.sort-it.net/how
Full of ideas on rethinking garbage and reusing things.

Every effort has been made by the Publisher to ensure that these websites contain no inappropriate or offensive material. However, because of the nature of the Internet, it is impossible to guarantee that the contents of these sites will not be altered. We strongly advise that Internet access is supervised by a responsible adult.

Glossary

Disposable—something that is made to be thrown away after it has been used.

Goodwill store—a shop that sells clothes, books, or toys to make money for charity. A charity raises money for a good cause.

Landfill site—a huge hole in the ground that is filled with garbage, then the garbage is covered with soil.

Material—the substance something is made from. For example, paper is made from a material called wood.

Packaging—bottles, jars, cartons, boxes, bags, wrappings, and containers. All these things can be made from different materials, such as paper, glass, and plastic.

Pollute—to make something dirty or poison it.

Answers to quiz on page 26–27: 1—the chicken is made from plastic bags and other pieces of plastic; 2—a rubber boot has been reused as a plant pot; 3—soda cans have been chopped up to make a ship; 4—this drinking glass is made from a glass bottle; 5—this bag is made from orange drink cartons; 6—this animal picture is made from old pieces of fabric.

Index

About this book

Making a Difference: Reusing Things aims to encourage children to think about garbage, to get the most out of different materials, and to have fun by reusing them in a variety of ways.

Reusing things is a good way to reduce the amount of trash that is sent to be buried in landfill sites. Encourage children to think about the consequences of continuing to send huge amounts of garbage to be buried every day.

Use **pages 10–11** to discuss how paper is made so children can appreciate its value and why it is important not to waste it.

Pages 12–13 encourage children to think of ways of reusing household items.

Pages 14–21 look at a range of different ways to reuse things. Repairing and repainting helps children value the time and energy used to make things.

Use **pages 22–23** to think about plastic bags and why the reusable alternatives are better.

Page 24 focuses on throw-away or disposable items. Discuss with children why it might be better to choose to reuse.

The quiz on **pages 26–27** encourages children to think about materials, to notice similarities and differences, and to see how they can be reused creatively.